LORD
of my
days

by FRANK TOPPING

Illustrations by Noeline Kelly

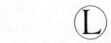

THE LUTTERWORTH PRESS
CAMBRIDGE

**To my mother and father
With love** .

By the same author: *Lord of the Morning*
Lord of the Evening
Lord of my Days
Working at Prayer
Lord of Time
The Words of Christ
Pause for Thought
Wings of the Morning

The Lutterworth Press
P.O. Box 60
Cambridge CB1 2NT

British Library Cataloguing in Publication Data

Topping, Frank
Lord of my days.
1. Prayer-books
I. Title
242'.8   BV245

ISBN 0-7188-2473-3

First published 1980
Reprinted 1981, 1982, 1987, 1991

Printed in Great Britain by the
Guernsey Press Co. Ltd., Guernsey, Channel Islands.

CONTENTS

PRAYING

Lord of my days
I have so often said, 'Teach me to pray.'
As a child I learned the prayer of prayers,
The Lord's Prayer.
I committed to memory
The great traditional prayers of the church.
They have been a foundation
And support for all my prayers.
But there are times when words fail me,
When all the prayers I've ever heard or read
Seem inappropriate,
And the jumble of thoughts,
Worries, questions,
Rushing through my head
Reduce me to silence,
Or the single plea,
'Lord, help me.'

Time has taught me
That I can pray without words.
You, who number the hairs on my head,
Know my every thought.

You know the decisions I must make,
Every problem, every failure,
Every triumph, every joy
Is known to you.
And it is enough to close my eyes,
To come into your presence and say,
'Lord, you know what is happening to me,
In my work, in my marriage,
In my mind and in my body.
Loving Lord, help me.'

Sometimes I have felt guilty
That I have not expressed my gratitude
For the love I have received.
But now I know
That I do not need to find acceptable words.
I need only be aware of you.
I see now that when music moves me to tears
It is because I have perceived your presence in the
    melody.
When, in a moment of drama,
Or at the peak of an artist's performance,
I feel a shiver running down my spine,
It is because your Spirit is passing through me.

A peal of warm-hearted laughter
Is a response to your love
Living in people,
And now at last I dimly see
That prayer is not only words
But a way of living,

An awareness of your presence,
A perception of the power of your Spirit in my life;
Supporting me,
Healing me,
Loving me.
Lord
Teach me to pray
With my life.

THE COMPANY OF HEAVEN

How many years had I looked
At sandstone rocks, red and soft,
Scoured by wind,
Engraved with lovers' initials and dates,
And never noticed that the earth beneath the grass
Was the same rich red.

I saw its redness that day,
Felt its coarse dryness in my hands
As we stood around and prayed.
Prayed with the wind on our faces
For the passing of my father.
The voice of the priest
Mingled with the breeze and birdsong
But in my head was the music of memory,
Voices, songs, stories
Sounding again and again in my mind,
And I knew
That he was not there,
Not beneath the flowers,
Not beneath the gaze of our bowed heads,
And yet he was with us
As he had never been before.
He, his brothers and sisters
And all the company of heaven
Reassuring us of a promise fulfilled.

In my Father's house are many mansions
And I go to prepare a place for you
So that where I am, you may be also;
If it were not so I would have told you.
And suddenly, in my mind's eye, I saw them,
Two tromboning brothers
Laughing whilst counting the rest bars
In the music of eternity.

The refrain was familiar
Yet I could not catch the tune,
And knew I never would
Not as long as I stood here
Or walked the journey of my days.
But the words, I knew,
At least the prelude to that unfinished masterpiece
Whose opening chorus begins,
The eye has not seen
Nor the ear heard,
Nor has it entered the heart of man
What things have been prepared
For those who love God.

And there
With that red earth beneath my feet,
I knew
That nothing could separate me
From the love of Christ
Or the love of those
Whose song, even now,
Is singing in my soul.

THE THINGS THAT LAST

People were living here
Before the Romans came marching past the
　　grocers,
The library and the bank.
The horse and ass and oxen
Pulled their weight through the gate in the wall
Where the buses change their crew.

Beneath the tarmacadam at your feet
You can feel the cobblestones
That broke the wooden wheel and the shoes
Of priest and tinker on their rounds.

The tallest and the oldest building still in use
Is the flying buttressed church
That suffered such abuse
From Cromwell's iconoclastic troops.

And all around are towers, tiles and chimneys
That felt the rain
That fell upon the faces of our parents
Before our days began.
Steps and stones,
Worn down brass plates
Declaring partners in law long at rest.

Windows and doors
Locking out and shutting in
The din of voices past and present.
Traders trade from market stall
To superstore with multi-level car parks.
In the street a meter-maid stands
Where silk-gloved hands assisted ladies
From their carriages.

Then as now
Men and women worried, argued and prayed
To a God outside of time
To whom a thousand years
Is but the twinkling of an eye.
Each of us in our short space
Will leave a mark.
The things we build,
From semi-detached to high rise flat,

May say something of our industry.
But the things that last
Cannot be measured in bricks and mortar.
For how old is sacrifice?
What age is faith?
How long does courage live?
When does hope end?

Lord
May the warmth and laughter and hope
That I have known
Be handed down in trust
To my children, and children to come.
May they live to know
That whilst all things fade and die,
Love lives on.

A ROSE IN A BOTTLE

Behold the lilies of the field;
Solomon in all his glory
Was not arrayed as one of these.

And behold a rose
Not in a garden
Or in some florist's artfully bound bouquet,
But in a bottle
A milk bottle in a kitchen
With the sounds of the dishes,
The radio and the children at breakfast.
A rose in a bottle
Startling among the cereals and marmalade,
As if in the midst of our domestic reality
A greater reality had sprung up
Between the salt and pepper and the butter dish.

Through the window is the garden,
Leaves and grass and roses.
Outside the window,
Beyond the cat washing his ears,
Is the garden I have seen so often
And yet so often do not see.
But this single flower
This rose in a bottle
Demands my attention.

Each velvet smooth petal
Softly curved and rounded,
Each subtle change of colour
From leaf and stem
To the depth of its bloom
Draws me closer
Until I am bewitched by the fragrance
That belongs only to this particular flower.
And there it stands between teapot and toast
Telling me that today
I shall not see anything more beautiful.

Lord
Let me not be blind
To the beauty I will see today.
Let me see the beauty
That I usually ignore
In people.
In between the queues for buses and trains,
In between the telephone calls
And the voices of friends and colleagues
Let me see beauty,
In words spoken with thought and care
In a job well done
In a single gesture of kindness.

Today you have shown me the beauty of a rose
In a bottle,
In an ordinary kitchen.
Let me see also the flower of love
That you have planted in ordinary people.

FIELDS

It's just a field
An English field in summer.
Beneath my head is grass,
Green and cloverleaf.
In my eyes and on my face
Dappled shadows,
Sunlight filtered through leaves of silver birch
Shimmering on a gentle breeze.
In my ears, the sounds of insects,
Grasshoppers, crickets,
Dragonflies and bees
Humming and hovering in heat and haze,
Exploring the hearts of flowers
Wild and sturdy in the hedgerows.
And in my head
The scent of fresh cut grass
Soothing the intrusive thoughts
Of a mind that never rests.

And it's just a field
An English field in summer.

A county, surrounded by mist grey hills,
Stretches like a patchwork quilt
Of greens and browns and golds
Stitched by hedges and lanes,
Decorated with cattle and sheep,
Knotted together with whitewalled cottages,
Farmyards and barns.

Deep, rural, harvest seedbeds
Pushing up from rain-rich soil,
Grain, corn, barley, oats and hay,
Filling the shelves of supermarkets,
The pantries of suburban semis.

Bread on the breakfast table.

Yet not by bread alone shall we live
Here in this field
Like the wind playing with the grass
Blows the Spirit.
The Spirit that brought forth the world
From the void of space,
The breath of life that feeds me
So that I shall never hunger.
In this very breath that I breathe
Is the mystery of all created things,
In this field
This English field in summer.

SKY

Lord of life
There is no part of your creation
That does not speak of the wonder of your being.
Day by day
We walk and laugh and live
Beneath the changing endless sky.
In cities, in countryside,
Or beyond the land
Where sea and sky marry
In mysterious union of height and depth,
Reflecting moon and stars and rising sun
When those with ears can hear
The sons of morning singing for joy.
And yet, how often have I missed
The songs of heaven,
With eye and mind tuned only
To morning news
And the fleeting hands of clocks.

Beneath the dome of heaven
The sky continues her dance
With shapes and changing colour.

From first light to dawn
The world is created once again from darkness.
Out of mists and shadows
The sun in splendour beyond the reach of kings
Breathes life into the world.
His feathered cirro-stratus train trails
Aloof to robust cumulus running before the bustle
Of the south-west wind.
And in the night
Stars stand sentinel until dawn.
Moonlight caresses hills, ships
And dreaming lovers
In the endless, everchanging drama
Played above the heads of people
Boarding trains, washing cars,
Buying, selling, sleeping unaware
Of imprisonment
Or the snare of smaller things.

Lord of all created things
Let me lift up my eyes just once this day.
May the passing problems of my waking hours
Be reduced to their proper size and place
Beneath the infinite sky.
May I know your presence,
Feel and breathe the breath of life
Which is your daily gift,
And may I see
In the beauty of the heavens
The measure of your love.

THE RIVER

High on a hill and looking down
I can see a river,
Wide and meandering,
Straddled by bridges,
Alive with all kinds of craft.

Sailing boats, motor-boats,
Pilot boats, police launches,
Harbour Authority vessels
Manoeuvering with all the grace
Of water-borne things,
Barges, lighters, coasters,
And cargoes of timber down from the north.

Flags that have fluttered
In Spanish harbours and Baltic ports
Fly over men speaking different tongues.
And the river bears them all
Swirling beneath their bows
Beer cans, plastic bottles
And all the flotsam of industry.

High on this hill
I can see the fields and green banks
That embraced the river in her youth,
And somewhere,
Beyond the rolling green horizon
The water rises in crystal innocence,
Sparkling over stones,
Dreaming beneath the willow
And listening to the thrill of meadow-pipit,
Lark and thrush.

Below me is my river, reflecting all my days
From the running, fresh quickness of childhood
To the slower, broader surge of strength,
Held in check by the ebb and flow of experience,
And beyond the estuary is the sea
And eternity.

Lord of life
Carry me through the river of my days.
Let me not be wearied
By an endless tide of demands
Or overwhelmed by the swirling pressures
Of the mainstream of my years,

But let me glimpse the enormity of your purpose
For every living soul,
And for me.
Let me live in the hope of your promise
That lies beyond the far horizon.

NOT A SPARROW FALLS

We heard them first
A whirring, rhythmic throb,
A steady beat of majestic wings
And suddenly
A squadron of swans,
Long necks extended,
Flew low over their reedy river.
We held our breath, pulses racing
In an excitement of joy and fear,
For they were both graceful
And menacing in their power.

Beneath them, unmoved,
A family of mallard ducks
Paddle between the reeds in the slow green water.
The shadow and sound of the swans fade.
Now we can hear the squeak and scurry
Of moorhens and coots
And see the surprised, indignant head
Of a crested grebe.
Swifts and swallows dive and dart
Feeding on the wing.
In the tree and out of sight
A robin sings a song
That is bigger than the bird,
Sweet and rich in pitch and variation.

Distantly
There is a continuous sound,
A rumble or buzz,
And it is hard to realise
That a mile or two away
Cars and vans and lorries
Are rushing into towns and cities;
That people are queueing and jostling,
Conveyor belts are endessly moving,
Whilst telephones ring
In shops, offices and homes.
We seem to be in separate worlds,
Unaware of each other.

Yet not a sparrow falls
Without my heavenly Father knows it.

Swans and geese and winding rivers,
Streets and lights and rivers of humanity
All fall beneath his gaze.
To him there is no secret world.

Not a sigh falls
Without he hears it.
Not a duck dives
Without he sees it;
Aches and pains are felt,
Birdsong is heard.
The miracle of the creator's love
Lies in his constant, caring presence.
No one ever weeps alone,
Worries alone,
Suffers alone,
Dies alone.
He who is aware of the meanest of his creatures
Has promised,
Fear not,
The hairs on your head are numbered,
And you are of more value than many sparrows.

REVERENCE FOR LIFE

In the first hour of light
When milk vans tour deserted streets
Purring like electric cats,
Breaking the silence with a clank of crates
Or the rattle of bottles,
Before alarm clocks shatter our dreams,
The creatures that live by meadow,
Hedge and riverbank
Have begun their struggle
To survive another day.

Otters begin their river patrol,
Deer, sensitive and alert,
Step their delicate way to secret pools.
Moles, voles, hares and rabbits
Sniff the air for warning signs of danger
Before scurrying to forage for food and drink.
Skylarks sing and eagles soar,
Black-backed gulls glide over sea and cliff,
Dippers dip and waders wade in fen and marsh.

Herons begin their morning walk
For all the world like elderly clerics
Hands clasped behind their backs
Deep in godly conversation.

And everything that moves and breathes
And flies, or walks or swims,
Is ours, our responsibility.
What is man that thou art mindful of him?
Yet thou hast given him dominion
Over the birds of the air
And the beasts of the field,
Yea, over every living thing.
But is a battery hen a living thing
Or merely a machine for making money?
Is a whale the greatest mammal of the oceans
Or simply a source of oil and fats?
Lord, forgive us for the blindness
That rips out hedgerows
Poisons the air
Pollutes our rivers
Plasters beach and bird
In the name of progress or profit.

You have made us stewards,
Entrusted us with the wonders of your creation.
Help us.
Instil within our minds
A reverence for every living thing
Lest in the hardness of our hearts
We lose our reverence for life itself.

ON THURSTASTON HILL

When we were boys we cycled to Thurstaston
Where the common was wild with shrubs
And purple flower and red sand rock.
Knights, come to the jousting field,
Our armour, flannel and tweed
With leather patched elbows;
Our helmets, peaked caps
Emblazoned with a grammar school badge.

Chase and skirmish filled the long afternoon
'Til weary of battle
We made the ascent
To the top of Thurstaston Hill
To stand like breathless conquerors
And stare across the estuary of the Dee
To the blue mists of Wales and its northern
    mountains.

Up on this hill
Where clean wind flipped our ties over our
    shoulders,
We were free,
Free from the trammels of theorems and French
    verbs,
Free from the tyranny of detentions
And six of the best.

Somehow, the wind on the hill
Filled us with an exultation
That could not be contained,
And we released it
By throwing back our heads and laughing.
Since then
The hills have shown me, again and again,
The proper size of the world below.

Not for nothing
Are there monasteries in mountains,
Nor was it by chance
That Christ climbed the hills
To struggle with his spirit
And bring order to his mind.
God forgive me
When I cannot lift my thoughts
Above the lowness of petty debate.
Forgive me
When I allow my mind
To linger in the marshlands
Of anger or suspicion.

Forgive me
That I cannot rise above attempts
To score off my friends,
When I fail to resist a base desire
To return blow for blow over some trivial matter.
Forgive me
When I allow myself to be depressed
By wallowing in the misfortune of a passing day.

I learned the lesson as a child
On Thurstaston Hill,
And it is not less true now.
In my heart I know
That when I lift up my eyes to the hills
I feel in my face a wind,
Fresh with love, alive with hope.
A wind that blows through worries
And leaves behind such a sense of the ridiculous
That once again, I am a child on a hill
Laughing in your presence.

ON A BEACH

On summer's day on every beach
From Blackpool to Bognor,
From Brighton to Bridlington,
The British paddle in the sea,
Make sandcastles and lie in deckchair ease
To the sound of breakers, seagulls
And shouting, squealing infants
Catching crabs in rocky pools,
Or digging channels
In vain attempts to stem the sea.

So many faces, yet so familiar.
Eyes hazel or blue;
Hair, blonde, brown or black;
Skin, fresh, freckled, pink,

Or darkest brown,
All reminding me of friends and family.
She could be my grandmother,
In profile that could be my Uncle George,
That voice sounds like my sister,
That walk belongs to cousin Jack.
All of us are related
Not in looks alone but in our lives,
Our fears and anxieties, our hopes and dreams,
Our passions, our pains, our pleasures.
Oh, some have better beach chairs
Or more expensive clothes,
And some have bigger mortgages,
Their faces tell you that.
Some have found the going hard,
You can see it in their eyes;
Yet, on a summer's day
We share the air, the sand and sea.
Individuals, yet united
In our frail humanity.

Why do I think I am special?
How did I come to think
That the world revolved around me?
I am never alone in any experience.
If I feel pain, so do millions more.
If I am anxious about my children,
Or money, or work,
Why do I hug it to myself
And think that life has singled out me
For special treatment?

Lord, help me to use my trials,
My needs, my failures, my successes,
My gifts, perhaps especially my suffering,
Not to measure myself
But to understand, to love,
To be able to share in the same struggles
That those around me are living through.
For the people on this beach
Are not distantly related to me –
We are all brothers and sisters,
Brown, black, blonde and pink.
Our only purpose
Is to learn to live in love
As children of God.

THE SILENT WITNESSES

Every year I see a miracle.
A dry, dead-looking bunch of twigs
Knarled and old throughout the winter,
An ancient, derelict bush,
Slowly
Comes to life again.

In April or May there are tiny buds
Whose tips show faintly green
On the withered branches.
As May advances on June
Fresh, clean, green leaves reach for the light.
In July I can no longer see
The horny old sticks of its skeleton
For they are covered with leafy finery.
In August, huge, pale purple blooms
Lift their heads to the sun
In final triumph over the dead days of winter.

My bush, my back-garden miracle
Is only one of thousands of millions
Of resurrections,

Throughout the country
In towns and cities,
In streets, parks and fields
There are thousands and thousands
Of silent witnesses to the mystery of creation.
Every bush, tree, blossom, fruit, nut and berry
Soundlessly shouts, 'See, I live!'

All around us is a great army
So quiet, so numerous, so common,
That we do not see them.
Apple, plum, pear and cherry;
Hazel nuts on wild hazel hedges,
Conkers high on horse-chestnut branches,
Sweet chestnuts to roast in winter,
How is it that we do not hear
Every leaf and branch singing songs of praise?
Exotic tulip trees, stately ash
And aspen, the quivering tree;
Copper beech, silver birch and fir;
Oak, the monarch of the forest
Who from humble acorns gave the timber
That floated Nelson's navy.
Churchyard yews, reaching back
In supple strength
To the long-bows of Agincourt.
Tree after tree has watched battles being fought,
Sheltered fugitives and lovers,
Seen the pain and joy of generations
And covered their years with autumn after
    autumn.

Lord, in my short and hurried day
May I pause for long enough to touch a leaf,
Or breathe the fragrance of a flower.
And in that moment
May I be in quiet communion
With your endless, life-giving love.

THE WEEDS OF TIME

In cracks and grooves,
Beside the thundering wheels of trains,
Grass and weed and wild flowers
Reach down into untended earth.
Hardy and tough they defy
The grey of steel and concrete
With gentle greens and blues and yellows.

Derelict houses, ruins of abbey and castle
Are softly clothed by creeper and clover,
Nettle and old man's beard,
Until, in time, only a grassy mound
Remains to remind us of the passing power of
    man.

Golden fields rich with harvest
Have heard the roar of cannon
And the cries of mortal combat.
Gentle pools and lakes
Cover places where, in sweated labour,
Men have gouged the earth
For clay and chalk and lime.
Warriors and conquerors
Built fortresses and towers
In their brief glory;
Yet the sun has set on all their labours
And grass and weed and tree and shrub
Have reasserted their claim to hold the land.

Lord
My day is very brief
And my sight is short.
A thousand years in your sight
Is like the twinkling of an eye,
For you are the infinite creator.
You dwell in eternity,
You are the beginning and the end.
Yet you have made me in your image.
You call me to enjoy eternity with you.

To you there is no past, or future,
All is one.
The saints who have gone before
And those who are yet to come
Are all part of your kingdom
Where everything that is good
And true and lovely
Is gathered into eternity.

Lord
Each day I live
Is another opportunity
To do something beautiful
For your eternal world.
Help me to see
That an act of love or kindness,
However small or simple,
Will never rust or decay
Or be covered by the weeds of time.

AN AUTUMN PRAYER

In such a place I could not speak
For leaf and lichen declared this holy ground,
A sanctuary.
Sweet chestnuts were falling,
Green, prickly spheres
Bursting apart on leaf-layered earth.
Acorns, pale and immature,
Spattered the ground around the oak.
My shoes depressed
The rain-soaked moss and glistening grass,
Footsteps hushed in the stillness of the trees.
Until, passing through
I came into the open
And like a rich symphonic chord falling on the
    ears,
My eyes were assailed with colours that sang
Chromatic scales of gold, and yellow and amber.
Leaves of brown and red and green
Raised praise to their creator
For the gift of deep and mellow autumn.

And it was lavish,
As the love of God always is.
This nature is his nature,
Extravagantly generous.
Like autumn leaves his blessings fall
And all creation
Acknowledges the love that never dies.
Only the blind of heart and mind
Cannot or will not,
See the love that wept
And hung upon a tree.

Lord
Let me reflect the colours of your love.
Let my life be bright with laughter,
My speech be gentle,
My thinking warm,
My actions kind.
May all I suffer or enjoy,
In the spectrum of my days,
Mellow and blend
In peace
In love
In praise.

A LIGHT IN THE DARK

The breeze died to a whisper,
Sails flapped, listless,
And the wind was gone.
Not a ripple remained
On the surface of the sea.
The little ship drifted
On a smooth, gently rolling surface
With her mast mirrored in the water,
An undulating reflection.
All around was silken serenity
Like an inland lake.
Yet the shores of this vast pool
Lay beyond our vision.

Even from the crosstrees of the mast
Nothing would be seen.
We took in the sails
And before the drift of the sea
Took us far off course
Started the engine
And put-put-puttered towards the horizon.

As darkness came we stared ahead
Hoping to sight a conical buoy,
A mariner's signpost.
But with darkness came the wind.
Hoisting sail we shut down the engine
And heard again the chuckle of the sea
Against the hull,
Saw the phosphorescent gleam
Of water broken by our bow.
Until then we had felt alone
But now, far off,
We could see the winking lights
Of fellow travellers,
Green and red and masthead white.
The wind backed and raced down on us.
Holding the squall in her sails
The ship leaned on her shoulder
And plunged into the waves
Throwing foam white water over the foredeck
And we pitched into the night.
For hour after hour we struggled
With sails and wind and sea.
Somehow we missed the flashing light

That would have fixed our place
In this wild night.
We feared that we were lost,
Had made an error in our reckoning,
And behind a façade of firm-faced confidence,
We prayed, and worked,
Until we saw the light.
Not the one we were expecting,
But another, greater light
That marked the land, havens and rest.

And there always is a light
As we plot our way through weeks and years,
Through the storms of our calling,
Through failure and disappointment,
Even in the dark nights of suffering,
Even in the face of death,
We pray, and there is light,
A greater light than we expected,
Guiding us to havens and to rest.

THE RHYTHM OF
NATURAL THINGS

There was a time
When man fell on his knees
And worshipped the sun.
There was a time
When the awesome grandeur
Of towering mountains
Made men pay homage
To a God of hills and peaks,

And those who ventured on the sea
Saw the terrifying power
Of the God of the vast and endless deep.
The earth itself could play with men,
Could graciously deign
To flower with fruit and corn,
Milk and honey,
Or turn towards them a barren face
Hardened with the merciless gaze
Of drought and famine.
So men made sacrificial tribute to mother earth
And prayed to her for a favourable harvest.

Primitive, unsophisticated man,
Yet was he nearer the truth than he knew?
I speak of him
As if I had never been moved by mountains,
Never felt that primeval stirring, deep inside,
At the sight of a majestic sky.
Never shivered at night, far from land,
On a moody, darkly surging sea.
Never felt the prickly fear of things invisible.

The Word was made flesh and dwelt amongst us,
And the Word was with God and the Word was
    God.

In a particular year, the Word took flesh.
Yet that Word existed, and exists
Outside of time, before time;
And moon and stars and earth and sea

From which we may have emerged,
The whole of creation
Is an expression of the nature of God.
And the simple seed that dies
And lies in autumn soil
To rise to life in spring
Is an echo of the Word of God.

Lord
Let me not be so removed
From the rhythm of natural things
That I fail to hear you
Speaking to me in the wind;
So cushioned by mechanical comforts
That I fail to feel your power
In the warmth of the sun.
So bedazzled by the brilliance
Of man's invention
That I fail to see your light in a morning sky.
Lord
Grant me the wisdom of the mind of man,
But keep within me the heart of a child.

LAUGHTER

At nine and a half
Though claiming 'nearly ten',
In a boating pool in Rhyl,
I learned a lesson about friendship,
About a certain kind of laughter
And something about boats and water.
I learned how to row
And caught several crabs;
Discovered the consequence
Of balancing with one foot on land
And the other in a boat.

That was when they laughed,
As I stood in the mud,
Grey flannel shorts wet and clinging,
Sodden socks that squelched beneath my toes
And a face crimson with shame.

I heard their laughter,
Or at least a noise that sounded like laughter.
A noise that mocked and jeered
And fell upon my ears
With the strength of blows.
Yet, amid the guffaws and cackles of derision,
One face looked down with nine year old concern,
One hand reached out to help me up the bank,
And then he smiled the smile of a friend
The rueful smile that said,
'Hard luck.'

I have heard, since then,
So much laughter,
Seen so many smiles;
Scornful laughs, sarcastic smiles,
Titters, sniggers and snorts,
Heads thrown back in sheer delight,
Tears of joy
And the honest open laughter
Of those who saw the funny side of themselves.
But of all the hoots and giggles
I doubt if I shall ever see
A smile more welcome
Than the grin that said,
'Whatever happens, I am your friend.'

Lord
As I speak and listen
Let me not laugh at another's expense,
Or smile at innuendo of gossip or malice.
Let me never misuse my sense of humour.
Let me be loyal to friends even in laughter.
Humour is a gift,
A kind of safety valve;
Let me use it wisely.
Let all my laughing and joking
Be open and kind and grateful.

WHO IS LISTENING?

I saw two people walking,
Talking with great animation,
Both of them speaking at the same time.
Could they hear each other,
Or were they just talking and not listening?
Would one say tomorrow,
'But I *told* you, yesterday,'
And the other reply,
'Did you? I don't remember that.'

Beneath the chatter and the flow of clichés
About the weather,
The football and last night's TV,
Are people saying things
That I do not want to hear?
Beneath the banter of lunchtime,
Are cries for help drowned in the coffee?
Is there a scream I cannot hear
Behind the tired smiles
And the shouts of
'See you in the morning'?

Friends talk, without hearing.
Committees talk, and no one listens.
Families talk, and no one pays attention.
The lonely weep, but their neighbours are deaf.
In the High Street
God himself speaks of his love.
Every day he offers eternal life
But his voice is lost
In the roar of the traffic.

Lord
Forgive me
That I choose not to hear
The voices that disturb me.
Help me to hear when someone sighs,
To notice a face, see the eyes
To be aware, to be sensitive
To the silent shout of a friend in need.
Teach me
To hear *between* the words.
Open my inward ear
So that I will hear your voice
When you speak to me.
Remind me, again and again,
That you are always listening.

THERE BUT FOR THE GRACE OF GOD . . .

In the news today
There will be stories of people in trouble,
People who have met failure
At some point in their lives,
And we who hear and read
Will make judgements.
It is so easy for me
To shake my head in disapproval
When I have not had the same temptations
Or met the same problems.
Who am I to judge another?
I do not know
What pressures, what suffering,
Others have had to face.
But I do know
That there is a hair's breadth
Between success and failure.

Deep down I know
That there, but for the grace of God, go I.

Lord
Today, if I hear something
About a friend or colleague,
Prevent me from making a judgement that is
    unkind.
If I read in the paper
About the mistakes of a fellow man or woman,
Do not let my mind turn to gossip.
Help me to see the best in people,
To hate the sin but love the sinner;
For there is no one who is beyond redemption,
Or beyond your love;
And when I hear opinions,
May I remember that they are *only* opinions,
For only you know the truth.

Lord, you have taught us
That love is patient and kind,
That love is never pleased
When others make mistakes;
But love looks for and rejoices in goodness.
Love does not want to expose faults.
Love always believes the best;
For love is always hopeful, always patient,
Love never gives up.
Teach me Lord
To make all my judgements
In the light of the love that never dies.

DREAMING

Daydreamer, where are you?
Your eyes are open
But focused on another world.
Your face is before me
But your mind is somewhere else,
Dreaming. Dreaming.
I do not know where your thoughts are,
But I know how the journey is made
For I am a fellow traveller
On the paths that lead to dreams.

Sometimes it's an escape,
A flight to happier times,
A visit to the past
Where memory has erased
All that was regrettable or sad
And preserved only laughter and happiness,
For memory is a comfort, a blessing

Where all the love, the conversation,
The days of sunshine
Are waiting to be re-lived.
Memory is a treasure store,
A casket to be opened with joy,
My own version of the truth
As it seems to me.

Or is it fantasy that I fly to?
Do the things I long for
Become reality in my mind?
Am I on a trip to the place
Where imagination rules,
Where what might be, is?
Building castles, sailing seas,
Making speeches in my head?
Have I inherited a fortune,
Won thousands of pounds on Premium Bonds,
Distributing with largess to family and friends,
Buying cottages with roses round the door?
Or do I dream of the attainable,
Of what work and thrift
And love and care might bring,
Of all I could give or share
With the people in my life?
For then 'dream' is another word for hope.

Lord
I am grateful for the dreams of memory,
For the wealth of good things remembered,
The source of comfort when days are lean.

I rejoice in the ability you have given
To live in worlds beyond my reach.
But this day turn my dreams to prayer,
To living hope
That the day will be blessed
With dreams that come true.
May this day be a good day.
May every smile be returned.
May conversation be without malice.
May my work be worthy of the gifts
You have given me.
May my friends be happy.
May the sorrowful be comforted.
May the hungry be fed.
May my sins be forgiven
So that I may rest in peace
To dream again.

THE FEAR OF LOVE

So many serious faces
In the shops and walking down the street,
Unsmiling, tight mouths,
An insular people
With secret thoughts, in secret minds,
Imprisoned, waiting to be released.
And the key that unlocks the warmth of humanity
Is as simple as a greeting or a smile.

I see my reflection in a window
And I wonder
Why am I so shut up within myself,
So withdrawn?
Am I afraid of other people,
Afraid to smile, afraid to talk?
Have I forgotten, or did I ever know
How to rejoice in simply being alive?

When people meet and exchange pleasantries,
The joy of their meeting
Stays with them for minutes after,
And then slowly
The shutters fall once again.

People who live in the same street
Do not know each other, do not speak.
People travel on the same train
In the same compartment,
Month after month, year after year,
And they could be in different countries.

If I cannot care and share
With those close to me,
How can I care for those who are far off?
Do I have some responsibility for the fact
That one half of the world
Suspects the other half?

Dear Lord
Forgive me for being afraid to love,
For being a miser,
Hoarding to myself the most precious gift I possess.
You did not fear to give your love,
To give and give again
Until there was nothing left to give
But your life.
Forgive me if I am afraid
To give a little time,
A little laughter, a little joy.
I am afraid of love
Because loving is giving
And I am afraid of the cost.
Lord, fill me with your love
So that I might share
The surplus of your riches.

TRAVELLING

Suitcase locked, pockets checked,
Keys, money,
Cheque book, credit cards, tickets.
Did I remember my tooth-brush?
Did I pack the book I'm reading?
Where did I put the asprins?
Time to leave.
Trains and planes and buses
Will not wait for my tooth-brush.
(I needed a new one anyway.)
'Cheerio mum.'
'Yes, I'll be careful.'
'I'll write.'
'I'll phone.'
'Bye-bye son, look after mummy for me.'
'Good-bye darling.'

There was a time
When a fourpenny bus ride to New Brighton
Was an adventure,
A ferry boat crossing of the Mersey river
An epic voyage to a distant land.
But now,
Fifty miles, a hundred, two hundred,
Is taken in a stride.
All the world seems to be on the move;
The air is heavy with after-shave
From faces glowing
Over pin-stripe suits and 'executive' cases.
Tweeds and twinsets tow cases on wheels,
And we wonder if those we love
Will look older.

Lord
You exist beyond the space we cannot cross,
Beyond the stars and planets,
And yet
There is no voyage made
Where you are not a fellow-traveller.
In all our journeys,
When we are weary, strengthen us,
When we are afraid, comfort us,
When we feel alone may we know your closeness.
At the end of the day
May we be united with those we love
And with you
Who are Alpha and Omega,
Life's beginning and journey's end.

CHRISTMAS LOVE

Once again
There is excitement in the air,
Holly and mistletoe,
Christmas trees, fairy lights,
And cards from forgotten friends.
Streets and shops possess a different feeling.

At this time of year
People seem to be laughing and talking
In grocers and department stores;
And everywhere there are carols.
For a brief week or so
There is love in the air,
Gaiety and warmth,
And all because of a child
Born long ago.

At this time of year
We are more generous,
We spend on gifts,
We make an effort to see family and friends.
We talk together,
Sing together, eat together,
Savouring the intangible wonder of Christmas.

Lord, at this time
Help me to spread my generosity
A little further,
Not necessarily with money
But with time and love.
You gave yourself
To the world for eternity,
Help me to give a little of myself,
If only for an hour,
To a neighbour who is alone.
Let me give a gift to a child in need.
Help me to let the love that is in my family
Overflow wherever it can.

Show me the ways in which I may share
The spirit of Christmas love.

As a child I wished
That it could be Christmas every day,
And grown-ups laughed;
But the love that came at Christmas
Is with us every day.
Lord I know I can be generous
With my love and time in this season,
So may your gift to me
Be Christmas love
That I can share
In every day of every season.

A LOVING WAY OF LIVING

In less time than it takes
For me to get to work,
In three quarters of an hour,
An aircraft can fly from England to America.
It seems beyond belief
And yet, we're told it's true,
A fighter that's faster
Than the missiles it fires.
We are living in an age of miracles,
Of jets and satellites, of rockets to the moon,
Of silicon chips, of computers and robots.
In my living room I can choose,
At the touch of a button,
Entertainment in living colour
Or international news of conflict and hunger
That shows we have not changed since Adam.

Throughout the centuries
We have not changed.
Our nature, our tempers, our passions
Are just the same.
Oh, we are clever in the things we can do.
Our hands and minds are skilful
In harnessing the energy of the universe,
But we have not changed.

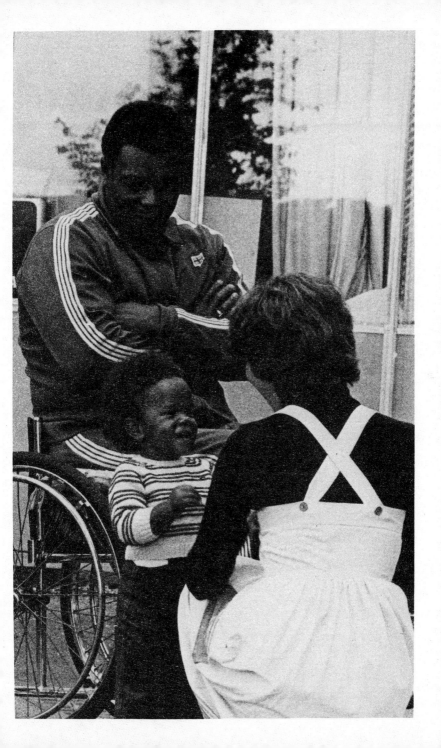

When men were covered in woad
And made their homes in caves,
Did they envy?
Were they jealous?
Did they steal or cheat or fight?
Where did they differ from those who live
In the semi-detached caves of suburbia?

Lord
You have given us immense power and freedom,
Above all
The power and the freedom
To choose or reject love.
Help me to choose
A loving way of living,
For only love can change
The things that matter.
Only love can change people
For love is at the heart of creation.
Love is of God.
God is love.

MORNING LIGHT

Looking through a window
With sleepy morning eyes
I saw an artist at work.
The early light
Tingeing sky pink and rose
Struggled through mist and cloud
And bathed my mundane view in mystery.
Rooftops glistening, wet with morning dew
Glowed with brief reflected glory.
In the miracle of morning
Back garden sheds,
Victorian bricks and sash windows
Are dressed in borrowed finery;
A precious gift from the rising winter sun,
A fleeting prize that must be captured
Before the greyness over-rules.

Beneath the rafters of every suburban house
Alarm clocks rattle, kettles boil
And razors fight their endless battle
With bearded chins,
Unaware of unheralded majesty
Passing silent overhead.
Days begin with breakfast
And the Lord of life
Waits without acknowledgement.

Lord of the heavens
Your light transforms
The skylines of cities and towns.
Forgive me for those days
In which the morning paper
And the wireless news
Take precedence over you.
Each and every day
You offer me the miracle of your presence,
The treasure of your love,
A loving presence
That can transform my life
If only I could be still
For long enough to receive your gift.
Lord, each morning,
Open my eyes
And let me live
In the light of your love.

WISE MEN

Wise men looking for a king
Were shown an aspect of a vunerable God.
Clothed in swaddling, love slept in a manger,
A simplicity which puzzles the wisdom
Of every generation;
For the personality of Jesus is not simple.
We cannot pin him down,
We cannot isolate him,
Pigeon-hole him,
Define him.

Gentle Jesus, meek and mild,
Stands beside
Jesus revolutionary,
Liberator,
Healer,
Priest,
King,
And brother of the poor and oppressed.
Jesus lives,
Not between the covers of theological volumes,
But wherever men and women gather in his name.

He cannot be confined to sanctuaries,
Churches or cathedrals;
He does not belong to political parties,
Yet he belongs to all who need him.
His wisdom is not our wisdom.
His love cannot be measured by our minds.
Yet his love is always within our reach.
Jesus said,
Come to me all you
Who are heavy laden,
With anxiety
With fear
With poverty
With sickness
With pain
With grief
And I will give you rest.

Dear Lord
Philosophers, theologians,
The wise men of centuries
Have tried to fathom
The depths of your being,
And in my small way
I have used the gifts you have given me
To explore your love.
Forgive me for the times
When intellectual pride
Has prevented my coming close to you.
Forgive me for allowing my cleverness
To come between my needs and your love.

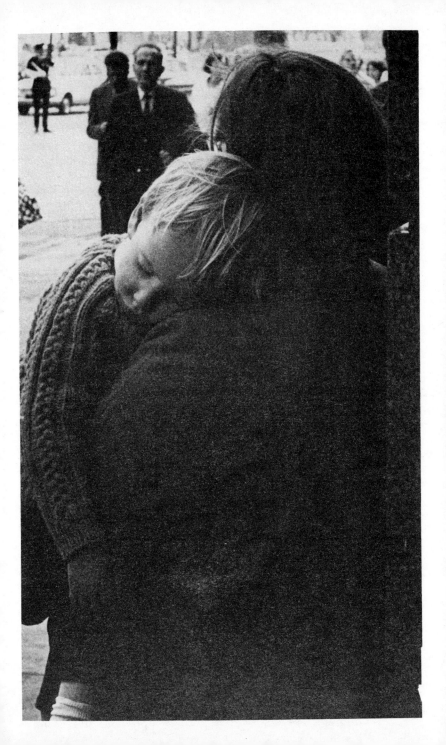

Forgive me for the times
When I have confused others
With the artfulness of my own words.
Lord, give me true simplicity,
Openness of mind and heart.
Remove the scales
That I have allowed to grow
Over my inward ear and eye.
Help me to see and hear
Your wisdom and your love.